THE ULTIMATE
KETO DIET BOOK

Affordable, Quick and Healthy Recipes for Everyone
incl. Exclusive Tips and Tricks for Weight Loss

[1st Edition]

Dylan Walsh

ISBN- 9781712454541

TABLE OF CONTENTS

3

EXCLUSIVE BONUS!

Get Keto Audiobook
for FREE NOW!*

*The Ultimate Keto Diet Guide 2019-2020:
How to Loose weight with
Quick and Easy Steps*

SCAN ME

or go to

www.free-keto.co.uk

*Listen free for 30 Days on Audible (for new members only)

The voices against eating excessive sugar and carbohydrates have grown so loud in the last few decades they have become difficult to ignore. Even though some critics may want to argue that the dangers attributed to foods high in sugars and carbohydrates are hyperbole created by scientists in the payroll of companies selling alternative diets, evidence that sugar is terrible for human health is mounting. This is not just evidence coming from businesses attempting to sell alternative foods; it is proof coming from credible institutions like the Harvard Medical School's Health Publishing. This has created debate about alternative diets like the ketogenic diet (referred to as the Keto diet). Adding to the discussion is that fact that celebrities like Lebron James, the American professional basketball player, Gwyneth Paltrow, American businesswoman, entertainer, and author, and Kim Kardashian, the American media personality, have been linked to the use of the Keto diet to get rid of access weight. This debate has led many to seek information about what the Keto diet is, whether it is safe and affordable for everyone, and what its benefits are. Others ask if it could aid weight loss and what role fats play in the diet. Those who want to start on the diet are also uncertain whether there are enough recipes out there for people who wish to follow the Keto diet strictly. These are issues we look at in this book, with the hope that by the time you get to the end of the book, you will have all the information you need to try the diet.

Apart from providing all the information you need as you prepare, start, and sustain a Keto diet, we have also included a total of 50 Keto diet recipes. The recipes cater for breakfast, lunch dinner, and desserts and snakes. Finally, some tips on how you can enhance your success with this diet. The book ends with a bonus 14 day Keto diet plan with a recipe for each day. It is crucial, however, to note that the keto diet needs to be assisted by other changes in lifestyle like constant exercise and reducing factors like stress in life.

What is the Keto Diet

For many people, the Keto diet means avoiding carbohydrates and eating only fats and proteins. However, this definition can be misleading because it could lead some people to believe that there is no space for foods containing carbohydrates in this diet. In essence, the Keto diet is an eating regime that recognizes the importance of the three primary macronutrients found in food: carbohydrates, fats, and protein. What then makes this particular diet different from all the other diets if people still eat the three significant components of food? The Keto diet seeks to prescribe the correct ratio of fats to carbohydrates and proteins. This is a ratio that aims to ensure that instead of converting carbohydrates into fats, the body converts the fats into substances known as ketone bodies (hence the name ketogenic diet). It is these ketones which are then used to fuel the body and the brain.

The Keto diet achieves its objectives by prescribing specific foods from which individuals should get their carbohydrates, fats, and protein. Carbohydrates are the starches, sugars, and fibres contained in foods like vegetables, grains, and fruits. Examples of carbohydrates recommended for the keto diet include the likes of vegetables, pasta substitutes, green beans, peaches, and carrots. Proteins are essential nutrients in the human body. They are mostly responsible for building the body tissue, repairing muscle, and assisting in the maintenance of healthy hair— bones, nails, and skin. Apart from ensuring the health of internal organs, proteins can also be used as a source of fuel. In the keto diet, recommended foods for obtaining proteins include the main types of meat like beef and chicken, fish, and cheese.

Fats, found in food can be divided into various types: saturated fats and unsaturated fats. Saturated fats are the unhealthy fats from foods like pizzas, margarine, and cookies. Saturated fats are the healthy fats found in foods like meat, and dairy products. They are also found in foods like avocados, vegetable oils, and fatty fish. The primary function of fats in the body is to support cell growth, provide energy, and protect the body organs. They are also essential for keeping the body warm. The type of fats recommended for the Keto diet can be obtained from foods like heavy cream, butter, vegetable oil, olive oil, and coconut oil. The Keto diet generally discourages foods like bread, cereals, pastry, potatoes, rice, and pasta.

The main aim of the Keto diet is to ensure that the body does not get most of its energy from carbohydrates but rather from proteins and fats. This is achieved by drastically cutting back on the carbs that digest more rapidly, such as sugar and bread. Generally, the recommendation is to restrict the body to less than 50 grams of carbohydrates a day so that the body does not have access to the carbohydrate fuel that it can use easily. Generally, the meals eaten by individuals on the Keto diet consist of between 70% and 80% fats, 20% and 25% proteins, and 10% and 5% carbohydrates. With a limited amount of carbohydrates to burn, the body is left with no choice but to start burning down fats and proteins. This leads to weight loss. The stage where the body reaches a phase where it starts burning fats and proteins for energy is known as ketosis.

In the majority of cases, the keto diet is suitable for people who want to lose weight. However, the diet has been linked to other medical conditions such as epilepsy, heart diseases, and acne. It is essential, though, to note that evidence on the effect of the diet on other conditions is still being gathered. This is the reason why it will be crucial to talk to a doctor before you start on the Keto diet, particularly if you have other health conditions such as type 1 diabetes, high blood pressure, and when you are breastfeeding. The diet has also been linked to assisting athletes in increasing their endurance, particularly cyclists and runners. This is because it can regulate the muscle-to-fat ratio, and makes it possible for the body to use energy more efficiently during more taxing exercises.

Variants of the Keto Diet

Even though the Keto diet is a strict eating regiment, individuals who wish to start on the diet can choose between various variations. For our purposes here, let's focus on four.

The Standard Ketogenic Diet (SKD)

The Standard Ketogenic Diet (SKD) stipulates that your diet should consist of 75% fat, between 15% and 20% protein, and between 5% and 10% carbohydrates. This variation has fats as a central component of all meals. When following this diet, the majority of your food will consist of the likes of butter, cheese, olive oil, fatty meat and fish, and avocados. Vegetables low in starch and fruits that are low in carbohydrates also have to constitute most of your meals.

The Cyclical Keto Diet (CKD)

If you want to follow the Cyclical Keto Diet (CKD), you will need to divide your days into keto days and off days. During keto days, you will follow the regiment you use with the Standard Ketogenic Diet (SKD). On off days, you increase your carbohydrates to 50% and then distribute your fat and protein intake evenly. When you follow this plan, you dedicate five days as your keto days and two days as your off days. It is still recommended that sugar should be avoided on off days. It would be advisable to select your off days with care so that you are free on specials days such as vacations or birthday celebrations.

The Targeted Keto Diet (TKD),

The Targeted Keto Diet (TKD), is recommended for individuals who want to follow a Keto diet but still need the fuel provided by eating more carbohydrates. This would be your plan if you are an athlete or have a manual job. Hence, your diet will consist of 10% to 15% carbohydrates, 20% protein, and 65% to 70% fat. The idea when following this variation is to ensure that the added carbohydrates you take are burned off as soon as possible.

High-Protein Keto Diet (HPKD)

Those who prefer the High-Protein Keto Diet (HPKD) often do so because it allows for increased amounts of protein. If you are following this variation, your meals will consist of between 60% and 65% fat, 30% protein, and between 5% and 10% carbohydrates. However, the challenge with this variation is that some people may not end up attaining ketosis. This is because it is much easier for proteins to be turned into glucose for fuel. However, because proteins take longer to digest than carbohydrates, weight loss can easily be achieved through an increase in the consumption of proteins.

The History of the Keto Diet

Even though the Keto diet is currently associated with weight loss, its origins and history are linked to the idea of diet as a cure for health conditions. The specific disease related to the diet is epilepsy. The history of the diet can be traced back to the early years of the 5th Century when reports were emerging that fasting was an effective method for curing epilepsy. This was also buoyed by physicians in Ancient Greece who supported the idea that restricting one's diet was an effective method of therapy against certain health conditions, especially epilepsy. At the centre of this lifestyle was what is referred to as "healthy fasting." This is fasting based on reducing the amount of carbohydrates in an individual's food and replacing them with, fat and protein, which ensures that the body burns ketones instead of glucose. It is for this reason that fasting would be the preferred method of treating epilepsy around the world for a period estimated to be around 2000 years.

Although the idea of using a specially designed diet as a means of therapy could be traced back to around the 5th Century, the word "ketogenic" would only be introduced in the first half of the 20th Century. This is the time when scientists started seriously looking at how they could replicate the biochemical effects of fasting. The initial research into fasting and its role as a therapy for epilepsy took place in France in 1911. This study concluded that epilepsy patients who combined fasting with the intake of low-calorie diets experienced a reduction in the number of seizures, and the effect of epilepsy on them was also reduced. It was also at this time that physicians in the United States, such as Hugh Conklin started recommending their patients to use fasting as a means of controlling epilepsy seizures.

In 1923, Dr Russell Wilder, of the Mayo Clinic created what is today referred to as the Classic Ketogenic Diet. This diet is centred on the consumption of four parts of fats for every single part of carbohydrates and proteins. The classic ketogenic diet is the foundation on which all the other variants of the keto diet are based.

As a method of weight loss, the keto diet started gaining traction around 1972 after the publication of a diet book by a medical doctor called Robert Atkins. In his book, Dr Atkins introduces a diet that is founded on the consumption of fats and as little carbohydrates as possible, creating a stage where the body enters the state of ketosis. Dr Atkins work started inspiring other scholars like the MIT–trained nutritional biochemist, Dr Stephen Phinney, to begin doing serious studies into how this diet can be useful for people involved in endurance sports. Soon, entrepreneurs like Robert Linn, an osteopath, were in the fold, creating what is called the Last Chance Diet. This extreme diet was based on drinking a mixture of fat and proteins until you shade any unwanted weight. However, there was a caveat: the process had to be managed by a physician. As can be expected, many people rushed in without the necessary supervision of the physician. This led to the death of about five dozen people, resulting in a lawsuit against Dr Linn.

Consequently stricter regulations were introduced regarding the use of the diet. However, Dr Phinney was not discouraged by these setbacks and continued doing research. He concluded that liquid ketogenic diets could still be useful as long as they contain enough minerals. It is based on these conclusions that the Optifast diet emerged in 1988. Like the Last Chance Diet, the Optifast diet contained enough minerals and vitamins. After it was endorsed by the America talk show host Oprah Winfrey, research into the Keto diet increased in the 1990s.

In 2018, the Keto diet was the most-Googled diet. What this shows is that the popularity of the diet keeps escalating. Today, studies into the diet generally seem to agree that it has beneficial metabolic changes, at least within the short term. Scientists are showing that apart from weight loss, other health benefits associated with a decreased weight such as high blood pressure, high levels of cholesterol and triglycerides, and insulin resistance are being noted. Scientists also agree that a Keto diet leads to reduced cravings for certain foods as a result of the high-fat content in the food, decreased insulin levels that promote fat loss, decrease in hormones that stimulate appetite as individuals eat fewer carbohydrates, ketone bodies reducing the feeling of hunger, and an increase in the use of calories because it takes more energy to convert protein and fat into glucose than is the case when converting carbohydrates.

Even though the positive effects of the keto diet have been well documented in studies, scholars involved in the research still warn that more studies need to be done as some adverse effects of the Keto diet have been suggested. These include an escalated risk of osteoporosis and kidney stones. Others note an increase in uric acid in blood levels (a factor that shows an increased risk for gout). Based on these risks, experts advise people on the Keto diet to ensure that they eat food with adequate levels of nutrients and minerals.

This is the reason why carefully selecting the foods you eat, when you are on a keto diet, should be taken seriously.

Weight Loss is Not about Counting Calories

Considering that the majority of people looking at the Keto diet as a solution today are doing so based on the need to lose weight, it is essential to look at the reasons why weight loss should not be viewed as just counting calories. The challenge with counting calories is that you are not basing your decisions on the quality of the food you it but rather on eating fewer calories. This means that you may still consume fewer calories from too many carbohydrates. If this becomes the case, then your body does not enter a stage of ketosis.

It is also vital for someone on a Keto diet to ensure that they include an exercise regime. This is because exercise stimulates the body to burn calories. For people on the Keto diet, exercise can especially be useful as fatty foods may contain more calories than the body needs. If they are not adequately made use of, these calories will soon be converted and stored as fat. Hence, people resorting to the Keto diet need to be cognizant of the fact that what is essential is to worry more about the food they eat as opposed to the number of calories the food contains. This is a way of ensuring sustainable weight loss and the health benefits associated with it in the long run.

Preparing For the Keto Diet

Just like anything in life, individuals starting on the Keto diet need to be prepared if they are to increase their chances of success with the diet. Instead of depending on your willpower, it is crucial to start by considering the lifestyle changes you will need to make. Start by learning as much as you can about the Keto diet so that when you start, you use the diet safely and effectively. Learning as much as you can ensure that you know how to set realistic goals and how you will track progress.

Ensure that you remove the type of foods that are prohibited in the Keto diet from your home. This will make it difficult for you to have such foods even when you crave them. Of course, it is essential to consider the other members of your family as you do this. Follow this by ensuring that making it easy to access keto-friendly foods when you need to snake.

Studies have concluded that dishing up food in smaller plates helps to reduce the number of calories you eat. One thing that you can also be assured will happen while you are on a keto diet is sweet cravings. Be prepared for them by stocking on keto friendly-sweeteners and having keto desserts available all the time. However, it is important to still ensure that you have to be strict about the number of calories you take even from keto-friendly foods. As long as you eat more calories than your body burns, you are not likely to lose weight.

It is also vital that you let the people you spend much time with know that you are embarking on the Keto diet. Inform them what this means so that they know what kind of support you need. If you believe that when you go shipping, you will be tempted by clever marketing gimmicks to end up with foods that are not in your list, enlist the service of a trusted friend or relative to do your shopping for you. Otherwise, you can shop online. If you have to go to the shops, avoid buying on an empty stomach.

Time: 30 minutes

Servings: 12

Fat: 11g

Protein: 10 g

Carbs: 1 g

Calories: 147

INGREDIENTS:

- ◆ 13 eggs
- ◆ 2 teaspoons chives
- ◆ 1 to 2 pinches Himalayan pink salt
- ◆ 227 g (8 oz.) Italian sausage
- ◆ ½ teaspoon garlic powder
- ◆ ¼ cup heavy cream

DIRECTIONS:

1. Prepare the oven by preheating it to 175º C (350º F) degrees

2. Until cooked through, brown the sausage and leave the meat to cool in the pan without draining the fat.

3. After cracking all the eggs into a large bowl, add all seasonings before whisking together into a consistent mixture.

4. Add the meat to the egg mixture and stir to combine.

5. Grease the muffin tins well and then distribute the mixture into the tins.

6. Bake for 30 minutes ensuring that the egg centres set.

7. Allow to cool and serve.

Time: 5 minutes

Servings: 1

Calories: 307

Fat: 30.81g

Protein: 6.6g

Carbs: 0.99g

INGREDIENTS:

- 1 egg
- 10g (0.35 oz.) butter
- 23g (0.81 0z.) organic mayonnaise
- Pinch of salt

DIRECTIONS:

1. In a non-stick pan, melt the butter.

2. Using a fork, mix the egg and mayonnaise.

3. In butter, cook the mayo and egg mixture.

4. Serve the egg and mayonnaise mixture into a serving plate and any excess fat immediately.

Time: 15 minutes

Servings: 3

Calories: 244

Fat: 23g

Protein: 5.5g

Carbs: 4.9g

INGREDIENTS:

- ◆ 4 eggs (organic and stored at room temperature)
- ◆ 2 tablespoons melted coconut oil
- ◆ 1 teaspoon vanilla
- ◆ ½ cup coconut flour
- ◆ ½ cup unsweetened almond oil
- ◆ ½ teaspoon baking powder
- ◆ ½ teaspoon Ceylon cinnamon
- ◆ ½ cup unsweetened coconut cream (ensure that it's the thick part of the canned cream)
- ◆ ¼ teaspoon Himalayan salt
- ◆ Coconut oil or grass-fed ghee for cooking

DIRECTIONS:

1. Apart from the ghee and coconut oil for cooking, combine all the ingredients and mix in a powerful blender.

2. Over medium heat, heat the skillet before coating the pan with just enough ghee.

3. Into the heated skillet, pour about half a cup of batter.

4. Cook one side until golden brown and then flip and cook the other side also until golden brown.

5. Set the cooked pancakes aside and continue cooking until the batter is finished.

6. Serve the pancakes immediately with your desired keto-friendly topping.

Time: 22 minutes

Calories: 248

Servings: 4

Fat: 19g

Protein: 16g

3.5g

INGREDIENTS:

- ♦ 4 large hard-boiled eggs
- ♦ 4 cups greens of your choice
- ♦ 8 large asparagus spears
- ♦ 8 slices bacon
- ♦ Lemon wedges (optional and use desired quantities)
- ♦ Berries (optional and use desired quantities)

DIRECTIONS:

1. Prepare the oven by preheating it to broil.

2. Using a single slice of bacon, wrap each asparagus piece.

3. Place each wrapped asparagus in a baking tray.

4. Broil for 7 minutes before flipping and broiling for another 3 to 7 minutes or until bacon is cooked to your preference.

5. Place a bed of salad containing hard-boiled eggs, barriers, and lemon wedges on a serving plate and put the bacon-wrapped asparagus on top and serve.

Time: 2 minutes

Servings: 1

Calories: 389

Fat: 32g

Carbs: 7.8g

Protein: 24g

INGREDIENTS:

- ◆ 2 scoops of Matcha MCT Powder
- ◆ 2 teaspoons of Vanilla Essence
- ◆ 2 teaspoons of Swerve
- ◆ 1 tablespoon collagen protein
- ◆ 1 cup coconut milk (freeze into cubes)
- ◆ ½ teaspoon Brain Octane Oil (Or other suitable oil of your choice)
- ◆ ½ teaspoon of your preferred sweetener to taste
- ◆ 1 teaspoon ashwagandha or adaptogenic herb of choice (optional)

DIRECTIONS:

1. Place all the ingredients into a powerful blender.

2. Blend into a consistent mixture.

3. Enjoy immediately.

Time: 20 minutes

Servings: 10 biscuits

Calories: 280 calories

Fat: 26g

Proteins: 8g

Carbs: 1g

INGREDIENTS:

- 3 cups fine almond flour
- 2 eggs
- 1 tablespoon baking powder
- 6 tablespoons butter, softened
- ½ teaspoon garlic powder
- ¼ teaspoon salt
- ¼ teaspoon xanthan gum

DIRECTIONS:

1. Preheat oven to 200 degree C (400 degrees F).

2. Place all the dry ingredients into a large bowl and mix.

3. Add the eggs and butter into same bowl and continue mixing into a consistent mixture.

4. Using parchment, line a large baking sheet.

5. After separating all the dough into 10 balls, create flat discs about the size of an average biscuit.

6. Put the discs in the sheet and back for between 12 and 14 minutes, ensuring the biscuits turn light brown.

7. Allow to completely cool so that the biscuits do not fall apart when you lift them.

Time: 30 minutes

Amount: 1

Calories: 603

Fat: 54g

Protein: 22g

Total carbs: 7 g

INGREDIENTS:

- ◆ 2 sausage patties
- ◆ 2 tablespoons sharp cheddar
- ◆ 1 tablespoon cream cheese
- ◆ 1 egg
- ◆ ½ teaspoon sriracha (taste)
- ◆ ¼ medium avocado, sliced
- ◆ Salt and pepper to taste

DIRECTIONS:

1. Using the instruction on the package, cook the sausages in a skillet on medium heat and then set aside.

2. Place the sharp cheddar and cream cheese in a small bowl and melt in the microwave for 20 to 30 seconds.

3. Mix sriracha and cheese and then set aside.

4. Make a small emulate after mixing the egg with seasoning.

5. After mixing the cheese sriracha with the omelette, put the sandwich together with one sausage patties on top and another at the bottom.

Time: 30 minutes

Servings: 5 (2 egg cups)

Calories: 209

Fat: 21.2 g

Protein: 16.3g

Carbs: 2.7g

INGREDIENTS:

- ◆ 10 slices bacon
- ◆ 225 g (8 oz.) mushrooms, sliced
- ◆ 6 large eggs
- ◆ 3 cups organic spinach
- ◆ ½ tablespoon olive oil
- ◆ ⅓ cup of feta cheese crumbles
- ◆ Salt and pepper to taste
- ◆ ¼ cup unsweetened almond milk

DIRECTIONS:

1. Preheat oven to 200 degree C (400 degrees F).

2. Wrap the bacon around the edges of each muffin cup and bake for 15 minutes.

3. Sauté the vegetables in a large skillet with the olive oil, starting with browning the mushrooms and garlic for about 5 minutes before adding the spinach and cooking for 2 minutes and then set aside.

4. Using a large bowl, whisk the almond milk and the eggs, seasoning with salt and pepper to taste and then set aside.

5. If the bacon has lost shape during the cooking, rearrange it so that there is enough space in the centre.

6. Distribute the vegetables in between the muffin cups, and then pout the egg mixture into each cup up to about halfway and sprinkle the feta cheese on top.

7. Bake for 15 minutes, allow to cool for 2 minutes and then remove from the pan by running the knife on the edge of each egg cup and then serve with a keto-friendly side of your choice

Time: 9 minutes

Servings: 2

Calories: 121

Fat: 6g

Protein: 7g

Carbs: 8g

INGREDIENTS:

- ◆ 4 cups cabbage shredded
- ◆ 2 eggs
- ◆ 1 teaspoon ghee
- ◆ 1 teaspoon apple cider vinegar
- ◆ Pinch of salt
- ◆ Pepper to taste

DIRECTIONS:

1. Place a large frying pan with a lid over medium heat and melt the ghee.

2. Add the cabbage and salt and toss in the melted ghee.

3. Cook over medium heat for between 3 and 4 minutes watching for the cabbage to brown.

4. Mix in the pepper and apple cider.

5. Separate the cabbage into two equal mounds and then create some space in the middle using a spoon where you will pour in the egg.

6. Into each mound, crack one egg.

7. Reduce the heat and cook until the egg yolks reach your preferred consistency.

8. Season with salt and pepper and serve immediately.

Time: 25 minutes

Servings: 4

Calories: 352

Fat: 22g

Protein: 34g

Carbs: 5g

INGREDIENTS:

- ◆ 4 bacon strips, crumbled and cooked
- ◆ 2 tablespoons butter
- ◆ 2 garlic cloves, minced
- ◆ 1 shallot, finely chopped
- ◆ 1 boneless ham stake fully cooked and cut into four pieces
- ◆ 1 cup Gruyere cheese, shredded
- ◆ 1 tablespoon minced fresh parsley, optional
- ◆ Pinch of coarsely ground pepper
- ◆ ½ pound fresh mushroom sliced

DIRECTIONS:

1. Over medium heat, place the skillet and melt the butter.

2. Add the shallot and mushroom, cook for 6 minutes or until tender and stir occasionally.

3. Add pepper and garlic and cook for an extra minute.

4. Remove from the pan and keep warm.

5. Wipe the skillet and then cook the ham for 3 minutes over medium heat.

6. After turning the ham to the other side, sprinkle the bacon and cheese and cook for between 2 and 4 minutes watching that the cheese has fully melted and the ham has been heated adequately.

7. Serve with mixture of mushroom and sprinkle parsley if desired.

Time: 40 minutes

Servings: 12

Calories: 338

Fat: 30.08g

Protein: 9.36g

Carbs: 9.74g

INGREDIENTS:

- ◆ 1 ½ cups almonds
- ◆ 1 ½ cups pecans
- ◆ 1 cup shredded almond flour (coconut flour is a suitable replacement)
- ◆ ¼ cup sunflower seeds
- ◆ ¼ cup water
- ◆ ¼ cup butter
- ◆ 1/3 cup sweetener
- ◆ 1/3 cup peanut butter
- ◆ 1/3 cup collagen protein powder (vanilla whey is a suitable replacement)

DIRECTIONS:

1. Prepare the oven by preheating to 150 degree C (300 degrees F).

2. Using parchment paper, line a large rimmed sheet.

3. Create course crumps out of the pecans and almonds using a food processor.

4. Transfer the mixture into a large bowl and then stir in the sunflower seeds, shredded coconut, vanilla protein powder, and the sweetener.

5. Melt the peanut butter in a microwave-safe bowl.

6. Over the nut mixture, pour the melted peanut butter and stir well, tossing lightly.

7. Stir in the water and clump the ingredients together.

8. Spread the mixture into the prepared baking sheet and bake for 30 minutes, stirring halfway through.

9. Remove from the oven and allow to completely cool before saving.

Time: 70 minutes

Servings: 6

Calories: 240

Fat: 19.9g

Protein: 6.4g

Carbs: 11.4g

INGREDIENTS:

- ♦ (All ingredients are organic)
- ♦ 4 scoops Vital Proteins Matcha Collagen
- ♦ 4 tablespoons coconut oil
- ♦ 4 tablespoons maple syrup
- ♦ 2 teaspoons vanilla extract
- ♦ I cup coconut butter, melted
- ♦ 1 cup coconut milk
- ♦ 1 teaspoon ground cinnamon
- ♦ ½ a cup hemp seeds
- ♦ ½ a cup shredded coconut

DIRECTIONS:

1. Blend all ingredients except the shredded coconut and hemp seeds in a high powered blender until they are smooth.

2. Place the mixture in a fridge for about 60 minutes or until firm.

3. Create 32 little balls from the mixture using an ice cream spoon.

4. Between the palms of your hands, roll the balls to make them smooth and set aside.

5. Create a mixture from the shredded coconut and hemp seed.

6. Roll the balls in the coconut/hemp seed mixture and ensure they are completely coated and serve immediately.

Time: 15 minutes

Servings: 1

Calories: 525

Fat: 58g

Protein: 19g

Carbs: 4g

INGREDIENTS:

- ♦ 2 tablespoons organic extra virgin olive oil
- ♦ 1 ripe organic avocado
- ♦ 60g (2 oz.) cooked smoked salmon, caught in the wild
- ♦ 30g (1 oz.) fresh soft goat cheese
- ♦ Juice extracted from one lemon
- ♦ Pinch of sea salt

DIRECTIONS:

1. Cut the avocado in half and remove the seed.

2. Chop the rest of the ingredients in a food processor into a coarse mixture.

3. Put the created mixture into the avocado.

4. Serve immediately.

Time: 25 minutes

Servings: 2

Calories: 454

Fat: 31g

Protein: 22g

Carbs: 8.8g

INGREDIENTS:

- ♦ 4 eggs
- ♦ 2 tablespoons coconut flour
- ♦ 2 cups grated cauliflower
- ♦ 1 tablespoon psyllium husk powder
- ♦ ½ teaspoon salt
- ♦ Toppings: avocado, smoked salmon, olive oil, spinach, herbs

DIRECTIONS:

1. Prepare the oven by preheating it to 175 degree C (350 degrees F).

2. Use parchment to line the pizza tray.

3. Except for the toppings, add all the ingredients into a mixing bowl and combine.

4. Place aside to allow psyllium husk and coconut flour to thicken up by absorbing liquid.

5. Pour the pizza base into a pan and mould it into an even round shape using your hands.

6. Place in oven and bake for 15 minutes or until brown and thoroughly cooked.

7. Remove from oven and place the toppings on the pizza immediately.

8. Serve warm.

Time: 50 minutes

Servings: 4

Calories: 621

Fat: 52 g

Protein: 33g

Carbs: 5g

INGREDIENTS:

- ◆ 225 ml (7.6 oz.) green olives
- ◆ 200g (7 oz.) shredded cheese
- ◆ 75g (2.6 oz.) cherry tomatoes
- ◆ 75 ml 2.6 oz.) Green olives
- ◆ 30g (1 oz.) parmesan cheese, shredded
- ◆ 12 eggs
- ◆ 1 teaspoon onion powder
- ◆ ½ leek
- ◆ Salt and pepper to taste

DIRECTIONS:

1. Prepare the oven by preheating it to 400°F (200°C).

2. After rinsing and trimming the leek, thinly slice it and then add to the greased baking dish together with pitted olives.

3. To a medium-sized bowl, add the cream and eggs and the larger quantity or the shredded cheese, and onion powder.

4. Combine by whisking and add salt and pepper.

5. Pour the egg mixture on top of the olives and leeks and then add the parmesan cheese and tomatoes on top.

6. In the oven, bake for between 30 and 40 minutes or until set in the middle and golden brown on the upper side.

7. If the casserole starts getting too brown on the sides before the dish is cooked correctly, cover with aluminium foil.

8. Serve as soon as you take out of the oven.

Time: 10 minutes

Servings: 1

Calories: 531

Fat: 52.71g

Protein: 9.21g

Carbs: 5.04g

INGREDIENTS:

- ◆ 80g (282 oz.) cauliflower
- ◆ 50g (1.8 oz.) Frankfurter
- ◆ 35g (1.2 oz.) mushrooms
- ◆ 28g (1 oz.) olive oil
- ◆ 16g sweetcorn
- ◆ 14g (0.5 oz.) butter
- ◆ ¼ Knorr cube dissolved in hot water
- ◆ 1 tablespoon GIA garlic paste

DIRECTIONS:

1. Chop the mushrooms, grate the cauliflower, and cut the frankfurters into slices.

2. Heat the Olive Oil and fry the mushrooms until brown.

3. Add the butter and stock cube dissolved in water and cook for one minute.

4. Stir in the sweetcorn, sliced frankfurters, grated cauliflower, and GIA paste and cook for two more minutes.

5. Season to taste and serve immediately.

Time: 45 minutes

Servings: 8

Calories: 325

Fat: 25g

Protein: 20g

Carbs: 5g

INGREDIENTS:

- ◆ 227 grams (8 oz.) Salsa Verde – Pace
- ◆ 4 large Green Poblano or Bell Peppers
- ◆ 4 tablespoons cream cheese
- ◆ 3 cups shredded chicken breast
- ◆ 5 tablespoons olive oil
- ◆ ½ cup mayonnaise
- ◆ ½ cup shredded cheddar cheese
- ◆ (The ingredients below are optional)
- ◆ Crumbled pork ribs for topping
- ◆ Tajin seasoning
- ◆ Fresh of pickled jalapeno
- ◆ Cilantro

DIRECTIONS:

1. Prepare the oven by preheating it to 220 degree F (425 degrees F).
2. Cut the peppers into half along their length and take out the seeds.
3. Place the pepper halves in a baking dish with the side that has been cut facing up.
4. In a mixing dish, mix the shredded chicken, cream cheese, and mayonnaise and any of the optional ingredients you are using.
5. Distribute the mixture into the peppers.
6. Drizzle the peppers with olive oil generously and top with the shredded cheese.
7. Place in the preheated oven and bake for between 20 and 30 minutes or until done to your preference.

Time: 30 minutes

Servings: 4

Calories: 430

Fat: 31g

Protein: 29g

Carbs: 7g

INGREDIENTS:

- ◆ 4 cups romaine lettuce
- ◆ 113 g (4 oz.) cheddar cheese
- ◆ 2 small limes
- ◆ 450 g (16 oz.) ground grass-fed beef
- ◆ I large avocado
- ◆ 1 cup chopped cucumber
- ◆ 1 teaspoon ground cumin
- ◆ I teaspoon salt
- ◆ 1 tablespoon garlic powder
- ◆ 1 medium tomato
- ◆ ½ teaspoon chilli powder
- ◆ ½ teaspoon pepper
- ◆ ½ cup cilantro
- ◆ ½ cup of preferred salsa

DIRECTIONS:

1. Under medium heat, place a coated large skillet (use butter, non-stick spray, or coconut oil).
2. To the pan, add the ground beef and all the seasoning and cook until brown, stirring occasionally.
3. Remove from heat and allow to slightly cool.
4. Use the lettuce, sliced avocado, cheese, and veggies to create the salad.
5. Top with the salsa, meat, and a liberal amount of lime.
6. Toss to combine before saving.

Time: 450 minutes (30 active)

Servings: 8

Calories: 656

Fat: 48.5g

Protein: 50.2g

Carbs: 1.4g

INGREDIENTS:

- ♦ 1600 g (56.5 oz.) beef shank or short ribs from pastured beef.
- ♦ 2 teaspoons ground turmeric
- ♦ 2 teaspoons ground coriander
- ♦ 2 teaspoons ground cumin
- ♦ 1 cup cilantro, chopped coarsely
- ♦ 1 teaspoon salt
- ♦ ½ cup water

Optional

- ♦ 4 garlic cloves (crushed)
- ♦ 2 teaspoons paprika
- ♦ 1 teaspoon chipotle powder

DIRECTIONS:

1. Combine all the dry ingredients in a small bowl.

2. Slightly coat each short rib piece in the spice mix before adding each of them into the slow cooker.

3. Over the ribs, sprinkle the garlic (if you opt to use) and cilantro stems.

4. Add the water carefully ensuring that you don't wash off the spices coating the meat.

5. On low, cook for 6-7 hours or until the meat falls off the bones.

6. Serve immediately with a preferred keto-friendly side of your choice.

Time: 45 minutes

Servings: 4

Calories: 420

Fat: 32g

Protein: 22g

Carbs: 11g

INGREDIENTS:

- ◆ 1 tablespoon vegetable oil
- ◆ 1 tablespoon sesame seeds
- ◆ I garlic clove, minced
- ◆ 1 green onion, sliced thinly
- ◆ 1 tablespoon fresh ginger, minced
- ◆ 450g (16 oz.) ground pork
- ◆ 1 tablespoon Sriracha
- ◆ 1 tablespoon sesame oil
- ◆ 1 cup shredded carrot
- ◆ ½ onion, sliced thinly
- ◆ ¼ soy source
- ◆ ¼ green cabbage, thinly sliced

DIRECTIONS:

1. Place a large skillet over medium heat and heat the oil.

2. Add the ginger and garlic and cook for between 1 and 2 minutes

3. Add pork and cook until the pink in the pork disappears.

4. Move pork to one side of the skillet and add the sesame oil, carrot, onion, and cabbage.

5. Stir to mix with the meat and add soy source and Sriracha.

6. Cook for between 5 and 8 minutes ensuring cabbage becomes tender.

7. Serve immediately with the sesame seeds and green onion used as a garnish.

Time: 60 minutes

Servings: 4

Calories: 923

Fat: 78 g

Protein: 42 g

Carbs: 10 g

INGREDIENTS:

Hamburger patties

♦ 650g (23 oz.) ground beef

♦ 75g (2.6 oz.) feta cheese, crumbled

♦ 50g (1.8 oz.) fresh parsley, chopped finely

♦ 2 tablespoons butter for frying

♦ 1 egg

♦ I tablespoon olive oil, for frying

♦ ¼ teaspoon ground black pepper

Gravy

♦ 175 ml (6.2 oz.) heavy whipping cream

♦ 30g (1 oz.) fresh parsley, coarsely chopped

♦ 2 tablespoons tomato paste

♦ Salt and pepper

DIRECTIONS:

For the hamburger patties and gravy

1. In a large bowl, add all the hamburger ingredients and blend with either your hands or a wooden spoon ensuring you don't over mix as this hardens the patties

2. Create 8 oblong patties.

3. Into a large pan, add olive oil and butter and then fry the patties over medium heat for about 10 minutes flipping over halfway to make sure that the patties cook entirely.

4. Whisk together the cream and tomato paste in a small bowl and then add the mixture to the pan when patties are almost done.

5. Stir and simmer for a few minutes before adding salt and paper.

6. Serve with vegetables of your choice.

Time: 60 minutes

Servings: 6

Calories: 344

Fat: 29 g

Protein: 33g

Carbs: 4g

INGREDIENTS:

- ◆ 4 garlic cloves
- ◆ 900g (32 oz.) lean grass-fed beef
- ◆ 2 tablespoons avocado oil
- ◆ 2 large eggs
- ◆ 1 tablespoon black pepper
- ◆ 1 tablespoon lemon zest
- ◆ ½ tablespoon Himalayan salt
- ◆ ¼ cup fresh oregano, chopped
- ◆ ¼ cup nutritional yeast
- ◆ ¼ cup chopped parsley

DIRECTIONS:

1. Prepare the oven by preheating it to 200 degree F (400 degrees F).
2. Place the beef, nutritional yeast, salt, and pepper in a large dish and mix.
3. Using a food processor or blender mix the eggs, garlic, herbs, and oil, ensuring that the eggs become frothy and the lemon, herbs, and garlic turns into a minced mixture.
4. Pour the egg mixture into the bowl with the beef and mix to combine.
5. Transfer the beef mixture into a small loaf pan and ensure the top is flattened out.
6. In the middle rack, bake for between 50 and 60 minutes, ensuring the top becomes golden brown.
7. Remove from oven and drain the excess fluids and allow to cool for between 5 and 10 minutes before slicing.
8. Before serving, garnish with fresh lemon.

Time: 30 minutes

Servings: 1

Calories: 594

Fat: 49 g

Protein: 33g

Carbs: 7 g

INGREDIENTS:

- 113g (4 oz.) whole mushrooms, quartered
- 113 g (4 oz.) steak
- 3 tablespoons chicken stock
- 1 ½ ounces cream cheese
- I teaspoon minced fresh parsley
- 1 tablespoon butter
- 1 large garlic clove
- ¼ teaspoon black pepper for the source
- ¼ teaspoon Worcestershire sauce
- Salt and pepper to taste

DIRECTIONS:

1. Over a medium to high heat, preheat skillet and add the butter.

2. Add salt and pepper to the stake and then sear before setting aside.

3. In the same pan, add the rest of the butter, and cook the mushrooms until soft.

4. After turning the heat to low, add the garlic and continue cooking for an extra minute.

5. Pour the chicken stock in and scrape the brown stuff at the bottom of the pan using a wooden spoon.

6. Mix the Worcestershire, cheese and black pepper in and stir until the cheese melts into the source.

7. Serve the steak with the mushroom stroganoff as a topping and the parsley as a garnish.

Time: 10 minutes

Servings: 1

Calories: 209

Fat: 5 g

Protein: 29 g

Carbs: 7 g

INGREDIENTS:

- ♦ 450g (16 oz.) fresh raw shrimp, peeled, cooked, chopped, deveined
- ♦ 1 large chopped avocado
- ♦ I cup cucumber, chopped
- ♦ ½ cup red onion, sliced
- ♦ ½ cup tomatoes chopped
- ♦ ½ teaspoon salt
- ♦ 1/3 cup citrus juice
- ♦ ¼ fresh cilantro, chopped roughly
- ♦ ¼ teaspoon pepper
- ♦ Olive or MCT oil for drizzling

DIRECTIONS:

1. Prepare and clean all the ingredients, devein, and cut the shrimp into pieces measuring between ½ and 1-inch.

2. Combine all the ingredients in a large bowl.

3. Serve immediately (it's also fine to keep the dish in the fridge to marinate and serve later)

Time: 20 minutes

Servings: 2

Calories: 231

Fat: 22.1 g

Protein: 4.45 g

Carbs: 4.23 g

INGREDIENTS:

- 42.5 g (1.5 oz.) cream cheese
- 1 nori wrapper
- 1 cup cauliflower
- 1 tablespoon coconut oil
- ½ medium avocado
- ¼ cucumber
- Soy sauce (for dipping)

DIRECTIONS:

1. Create the rice using about 1/5 head of cauliflower and then pulsing it in a food processor.

2. Over medium-high, heat the coconut oil and add cauliflower rice.

3. Cook for between 5 and 7 minutes, ensuring that the rice is fully cooked and then transfer to a bowl and set aside.

4. Make thin slices using the cream cheese, avocado and cucumber and set aside.

5. On a clean flat surface, lay down a long layer of plastic wrap, and lay the nori wrapper on top of the plastic wrap.

6. On top of the nori wrapper, lay down the cauliflower rice leaving a little room around the edges.

7. Add the avocado on the edge of the rice closest to you, add the layer of cream cheese on the avocado, and then place the cucumber on top.

8. Lift the plastic wrapper under the nori wrapper, ensuring the ingredients do not fall off until the whole thing is rolled.

9. As you roll, ensure that the plastic wrapper is not rolling inside the sushi. Hence, you would want to edge the plastic wrap off the nori as you are rolling.

10. Slice the sushi into 8 pieces using a sharp knife (start in the middle so that you are not pushing off the rice on the two open edges.

Time: 5 minutes

Servings: 1

Calories: 406

Fat: 37g

Protein: 17g

Carbs: 1g

INGREDIENTS:

- ◆ 142g (5 oz.) canned tuna
- ◆ 2 tablespoons red onion, finely chopped
- ◆ 2 cups romaine lettuce, roughly chopped
- ◆ 1 tablespoon lime juice
- ◆ 1 teaspoon chilli lime seasoning
- ◆ I medium stalk celery, finely chopped
- ◆ 1/3 cup mayonnaise
- ◆ Salt and pepper to taste
- ◆ (Optional)
- ◆ Black pepper
- ◆ Green onion, chopped
- ◆ Lemon juice

DIRECTIONS:

1. In a medium-size bowl, add lime juice mayonnaise, chilli lime, and pepper, and stir well until smooth.

2. Coat the vegetables and tuna by adding them into the bowl.

3. Serve with celery over greens.

Time: 25 minutes

Servings: 4

Calories: 815

Fat: 67 g

Protein: 47 g

Carbs: 7g

INGREDIENTS:

- ◆ 650 g (23 oz.) turkey breast
- ◆ 475 ml (17 oz.) crème Fraiche or heavy whipping cream
- ◆ 200g (7 oz.) cream cheese
- ◆ 75 ml (2.6 oz.) small capers
- ◆ 2 tablespoons butter
- ◆ 1 tablespoon tamari soy sauce

DIRECTIONS:

1. Prepare the oven by preheating it to 175°C (350°F).

2. In a large oven-proof frying pan, melt half the butter over medium heat and then season the turkey liberally and fry until golden brown on all sides.

3. Place the turkey in an oven to finish it off and once the internal temperature of the turkey reaches74°C (165°F), transfer to a plate and cover with foil.

4. Pour the drippings from the turkey into a small saucepan and then add cream and cream cheese before stirring to a light boil. Add soy sauce, and season with salt and pepper.

5. Sauté the capers until crispy in a medium frying pan with the remaining butter over high heat.

6. Serve turkey immediately with fried capers and sauce.

Time: 45 minutes

Servings: 4

Calories: 288

Fat: 23g

Protein: 29g

Carbs: 3g

INGREDIENTS:

- ◆ 4 boneless pork chops
- ◆ 2 tablespoons ghee
- ◆ 2 tablespoons sweetener
- ◆ 2 chayote, chop to ½ inch pieces
- ◆ 1 tablespoon cinnamon
- ◆ 1 tablespoon cider vinegar
- ◆ ½ teaspoon sea salt
- ◆ 1/8 teaspoon nutmeg

DIRECTIONS:

1. Place a large skillet over medium heat and melt ghee, add the pork chops and cook for 5 minutes.

2. Flip the pork chops before adding the chayote and sprinkling the apple cider vinegar, sweetener, nutmeg, and cinnamon.

3. Cook for 5 more minutes.

4. Take the pork chops out and set aside.

5. Allow the chayote mixture to a boil for a few minutes before reducing the low heat medium and simmer with cover for about 30 minutes.

6. Serve immediately with the warm pork chops.

Time: 20 minutes

Servings: 3

Calories: 336

Fat: 23 g

Protein: 29 g

Carbs: 6 g

INGREDIENTS:

- ♦ 6 slices sharp cheddar cheese
- ♦ 6 Portobello mushroom caps, remove stems, rinse and dab dry
- ♦ 450g (16 oz.) grass-fed ground beef
- ♦ 1 tablespoon Worcestershire sauce
- ♦ 1 tablespoon avocado oil
- ♦ 1 teaspoon Himalayan salt
- ♦ 1 teaspoon black pepper

DIRECTIONS:

1. Combine the Worcestershire sauce, ground beef, pepper, and salt in a large bowl and create burger patties.

2. Heat avocado oil over medium heat in a large pan.

3. Add the mushrooms and cook for between 3 and 4 minutes on either side before removing from heat.

4. Cook the burger patties for 5 minutes on each side in the same pan.

5. Add the cheese on top of the burgers and cover with lid to permit the cheese to melt.

6. Layer each mushroom cap, creating a cheeseburger, and then put in your preferred garnishes before placing the other mushroom lid on top.

7. Serve immediately.

Time: 20 minutes

Servings: 6

Calories: 332

Fat: 25 g

Protein: 20 g

Carbs: 9 g

INGREDIENTS:

- ♦ 227g (8 oz.) Romaine lettuce, chopped
- ♦ 2 tablespoons taco seasoning
- ♦ 1 1/3 cup Grape tomatoes, halved
- ♦ 450g (16 oz.) ground beef
- ♦ 1 teaspoon avocado oil (or any keto-friendly oil)
- ♦ 1 medium avocado, cubed
- ♦ ½ cup green onions
- ♦ ¾ cup Cheddar cheese, shredded
- ♦ 1/3 cup Salsa
- ♦ 1/3 cup sour cream

DIRECTIONS:

1. Place skillet over high heat and heat the oil.

2. Add ground beef into the skillet and fry for between 7 and 10 minutes while also breaking up the pieces using a spatula. Ensure the beef browns, and the moisture has reduced significantly.

3. Stir Taco seasoning into the ground beef until combined well and remove from the heat.

4. As the beef cooks, use a large bowl to combine the remaining ingredients and add the ground beef before tossing everything together.

5. Serve immediately.

Time: 26 minutes

Servings: 1

Calories: 500

Fat: 46g

Protein: 18g

Carbs: 5g

INGREDIENTS:

- ◆ 80g (2.8 oz.) broccoli, cut into bite-size pieces
- ◆ 70g (2.5 oz.) chicken breast, skinless, raw, and cut into small pieces
- ◆ 40g (1.4 oz.) heavy cream
- ◆ 26g (0.9 oz.) butter
- ◆ 8g (0.28 oz.) olive oil
- ◆ 5g (0.17 oz.) lemon
- ◆ Enough chicken broth to thin sauce
- ◆ Salt and pepper to taste
- ◆ Tabasco sauce to taste, optional

DIRECTIONS:

1. In a small pan over medium-high, heat olive oil and butter.

2. Add the chicken and sauté for three minutes, turning the chicken around occasionally to brown.

3. Turn the heat to medium and stir in the lemon juice, salt, Tabasco sauce, and black pepper.

4. Stir the chicken broth and cover the pan, turning the heat off and leaving the chicken and broccoli to simmer for about 10 minutes.

5. Serve immediately.

Time: 30 minutes

Servings: 2

Calories: 693

Fat: 62g

Protein: 27g

Carbs: 5g

INGREDIENTS:

- 225g (8 oz.) goat cheese
- 40g (1.41 oz.) baby spinach
- 4 tablespoons olive oil
- 2 Garlic cloves
- 2 tablespoons unsweetened marinara sauce
- 1 medium zucchini
- Salt and pepper to taste

DIRECTIONS:

1. Prepare the oven by preheating it to 190 degree C (375 degrees F).

2. Cut the zucchini at the centre along its length and remove the seeds. Keep the seeds.

3. Place the zucchini on a baking sheet with the cut side facing up.

4. Peel the cloves of garlic and thinly slice them and use half of the olive oil to fry the garlic over medium heat in a skillet until it browns a bit.

5. Add the zucchini seeds and baby spinach into the skillet and fry until soft, while also adding the salt and pepper.

6. Over the zucchini boats spread the marinara sauce and top with the fried garlic and baby spinach, sprinkle the goat cheese on top.

7. Place in the oven and bake for between 20 and 25 minutes watching for zucchini to become tender and golden brown.

8. Drizzle the rest of the olive oil over the zucchini boats.

9. Season with ground pepper and serve immediately.

Time: 40 minutes

Servings: 4

Calories: 460

Fat: 50g

Protein: 39g

Carbs: 1g

INGREDIENTS:

- ◆ 4 pork loin chops
- ◆ 2 cloves garlic, minced
- ◆ 1 tablespoon extra-virgin olive oil
- ◆ I tablespoon freshly minced rosemary
- ◆ ½ cup butter melted
- ◆ Ground pepper
- ◆ Kosher salt

DIRECTIONS:

1. Prepare the oven by preheating to 190 degree C (375° F).

2. Use the salt and pepper to season the pork chops.

3. Mix the rosemary, garlic, and butter in a small bowl and set aside.

4. Heat the olive oil over medium heat in an oven-safe skillet and add pork chops.

5. Sear until pork chops turn golden brown (between 3 and 4 minutes) and then flip and cook the other side for the same amount of time.

6. Use garlic butter to brush the pork chops liberally.

7. Put the skillet in the oven and cook for between 10 and 12 minutes.

8. Serve immediately after brushing with more garlic butter.

Time: 50 minutes

Servings: 4

Calories: 568

Fat: 40g

Protein: 38g

Carbs: 6g

INGREDIENTS:

- 2 Tablespoons coconut oil
- 1 can diced green chillies
- 454g (16 oz.) chicken thighs, boneless and skinless
- ¾ cup red enchilada sauce
- ¼ cup water
- ¼ cup chopped onion

Suggested toppings

- 1 whole avocado, diced
- 1 tomato, chopped
- 1 cup shredded cheese
- ½ cup sour cream
- ¼ cup chopped pickled jalapenos

DIRECTIONS:

1. Over medium heat, melt the coconut oil and sear chicken thighs until they start to brown.

2. Pour in the enchilada sauce and water and then add the green chillies and onion and then reduce heat and cover to simmer for between 17 and 25 minutes.

3. Remove the chicken carefully, and place on a work surface and then either shred or chop the chicken and put it back in the pot.

4. Simmer the chicken uncovered for another 10 minutes allowing it to soak in the flavour and permit the sauce to reduce slightly.

5. Serve immediately with toppings of your choice.

Time: 10 minutes
Servings: 5 (2 egg cups)
Calories: 459
Fat: 35g
Protein: 27g
Carbs: 3.5g

INGREDIENTS:

Pizza Crust

- ◆ 2 large eggs
- ◆ 2 tablespoons Parmesan Cheese
- ◆ 2 teaspoons frying oil
- ◆ 1 tablespoon Psyllium Husk Powder
- ◆ ½ teaspoon Italian seasoning
- ◆ Salt to taste

Toppings

- ◆ 3 tablespoons Rao's Tomato Sauce
- ◆ 42.5 g (1.5 oz.) Mozzarella Cheese
- ◆ 1 tablespoon freshly chopped basil

DIRECTIONS:

1. Mix all the pizza crust ingredients (except the frying oil) in a bowl using a blender.

2. In a frying pan, heat the oil and then place the pizza crust mixture in the pan and create a beautiful circle.

3. When crust edges start to brown, flip to the other side and cook for another 1 minute.

4. Turn the stove off and turn on the broiler

5. Add the tomato sauce and Mozzarella cheese and broil for about 2 minutes or watch for the cheese to bubble.

6. Garnish with basil before serving.

Time: 30 minutes

Servings: 4

Calories: 406

Fat: 19g

Protein: 28g

Carbs: 7g

INGREDIENTS:

- 2 tablespoons coconut aminos
- 2 teaspoons garlic powder
- 1 ½ cups Bok Choy, cleaned and cut into ½ inch slices
- 454g (16 oz.) boneless, skinless chicken breasts, cut into bite-size pieces
- 1/3 cup shallot, minced
- ½ cup raw cashew pieces
- ½ cup stalks celery pieces, sliced thin
- ½ cup coconut oil, full fat
- ½ cup fresh cilantro, chopped
- Salt and pepper to taste

DIRECTIONS:

1. In a large skillet, melt the oil and then add the celery and shallots (also add the garlic if you are using freshly minced garlic) and sauté until shallots are translucent.

2. Add the chicken and cook until it browns and then add the cashews, garlic powder (in case you are using garlic powder) and then stir in coconut milk.

3. Cook until the meat cooks through and the coconut has reduced into a layer as opposed to being a sauce.

4. Take the skillet off the heat and toss in the fresh cilantro and coconut aminos.

5. Add salt and pepper to taste and serve.

Time: 20 minutes

Servings: 4

Calories: 411

Fat: 19g

Protein: 46g

Carbs: 12g

INGREDIENTS:

- 450g to 500g (16 oz. to 17.5 oz.) chicken fillets
- 400g (14 oz.) crushed tomatoes
- 7 to 10 cherry tomatoes, chop into half
- 2 minced zucchinis
- 1 medium diced onion
- 1 garlic, minced
- ½ teaspoon coconut butter
- 100g (3.5 oz.) raw cashews
- Salt, basil, pepper, and dry oregano

DIRECTIONS:

1. Into a large pan over medium to high heat add the coconut butter and diced onions and cook for between 30 seconds and 1 minute, ensuring that the oil does not burn.

2. Dice the chicken into 2 cm pieces.

3. Add the minced garlic and the chicken into the pan and use the oregano, basil, salt and pepper and then cook chicken for between 5 and 6 minutes ensuring that it turns golden.

4. Spiralize the zucchini while the chicken is cooking (If you do not have a spirilizer, you can use a vegetable peeler).

5. Into the pan with the chicken, add the tomatoes and simmer for between 3 and 5 minutes.

6. In a separate pan roast the cashews until golden and season with turmeric, paprika, and salt.

7. Add the noodles and cherry tomatoes into the pan with the chicken together with the seasoning and cook for another 1 minute before turning off the heat.

8. Serve the zoodles with fresh basil and spiced cashews.

Time: 55 minutes

Servings: 4

Calories: 506

Fat: 34g

Protein: 34g

Carbs: 6g

INGREDIENTS:

- ◆ 500g (17.5 oz.) chicken thigh fillets, fat trimmed
- ◆ 1/2 cup pouring cream
- ◆ 55g (2 oz.) 3-cheese mix
- ◆ 10g (0.35 oz.) butter
- ◆ 2 rushers bacon, chopped
- ◆ 2 green shallots, trimmed, sliced
- ◆ 1 tablespoon olive oil
- ◆ I bunch English spinach, trimmed and chopped
- ◆ 1 small cauliflower

Optional

- ◆ 2 tablespoons fresh thyme leaves

DIRECTIONS:

1. Heat butter and oil in a pan over medium heat, add bacon and cauliflower and cook for 8 to 10 minutes occasionally stirring until golden brown.

2. Add spinach and cook for 2 minutes

3. Remove from heat and add thyme, cream, and half of the shallot and stir to combine before transferring into a prepared dish.

4. Wipe the pan clean and spray with oil, add the chicken, cook for 2 minutes on each side or until golden, and then place over the cauliflower mixture.

5. Sprinkle cheese around the chicken and then bake for between 20 and 25 minutes.

6. Allow to cool down for 5 minutes before serving and top with the remaining shallot.

Time: 85 minutes

Servings: 6

Calories: 431

Fat: 29g

Protein: 30g

Carbs: 7g

INGREDIENTS:

- ◆ 170g (6 oz.) shredded Cheddar (about 1 ½ cups)
- ◆ 4 Slices bacon, chopped
- ◆ 2 cloves garlic, minced
- ◆ 2 tablespoons sugar-free ketchup
- ◆ 2 tablespoons Worcestershire sauce
- ◆ I medium spaghetti squash
- ◆ 450g (16 oz.) ground beef
- ◆ ½ teaspoon salt
- ◆ ½ teaspoon pepper

DIRECTIONS:

1. Prepare the oven by preheating it to 200 degree C (400 degrees F) and lining the baking sheet with parchment paper.

2. Cut the squash into halves along its length, remove the seeds and back the squash for about 40 minutes.

3. While the squash bakes, cook the bacon until crisp in a large skillet over medium heat and then remove and place in a dish with a paper towel

4. In the same pan, cook the beef and break up any clumps using the back of a spoon.

5. After about 7 minutes, add the salt, pepper, and garlic, and cook for another 2 to 3 minutes.

6. Stir in the Worcestershire sauce and ketchup.

7. Scoop the flesh from the squash and mix into the ground beef.

8. Sprinkle Cheddar cheese on top, cover the skillet and reduce the heat to low and allow the cheese to melt.

9. Serve with the bacon sprinkled on top.

Time: 30 minutes

Servings: 4

Calories: 263

Fat: 16g

Protein: 26g

Carbs: 1g

INGREDIENTS:

- ◆ 2 tablespoons Dijon mustard
- ◆ 2 tablespoons water
- ◆ 1 ½ cups pork rind panko
- ◆ 455g (16 oz.) white fish
- ◆ ¾ teaspoons Cajun seasoning
- ◆ ¼ cup mayonnaise
- ◆ Salt and pepper to taste

DIRECTIONS:

1. Prepare the air fryer by spraying with non-stick spray.

2. Cut the fish into sticks of about 1 inch by two inches wide.

3. Whisk the mustard, mayo, and water in a small bowl.

4. In a separate bowl, whisk together the Cajun seasoning and pork rinds and then add the seasoning (taste first to determine how much you need).

5. Dip each fish finger into the mayo mixture and then into the pork and rind mixture and toss to coat and then put in the air fryer rack.

6. Bake for 5 minutes in an air fryer at 200 degree C (400 degree F) before flipping the sticks and baking for another 5 minutes.

7. Serve and enjoy with a keto-friendly sauce of your choice.

Time: 480 minutes

Servings: 6

Calories: 391

Fat: 25g

Protein: 31g

Carbs: 7g

INGREDIENTS:

- ◆ 455 ml (16 oz.) beef broth
- ◆ 410 ml (14.5 oz.) can diced tomatoes, un-drained
- ◆ 340 (12 oz.) package sliced mushrooms
- ◆ 4 Cloves garlic, minced
- ◆ 900g (32 oz.) beef stew meat
- ◆ 2 celery stalks, sliced
- ◆ 2 tablespoons balsamic vinegar
- ◆ 1 ½ white onion, sliced
- ◆ 1 tablespoon Worcestershire sauce
- ◆ 1 teaspoon salt
- ◆ 1 teaspoon garlic powder
- ◆ 1 teaspoon onion powder
- ◆ 1 teaspoon oregano
- ◆ ¾ teaspoon pepper
- ◆ ½ of white onion

DIRECTIONS:

1. Place all the contents into a freezer bag and cook in a slow cooker together with the broth and cook on low for 8 hours until meat is tender.

2. Serve with keto-friendly vegetables of your choice.

Time: 480 minutes

Servings: 6

Calories: 392

Fat: 23g

Protein: 42g

Carbs: 3g

INGREDIENTS:

- ◆ 170 (6 oz.) chicken broth
- ◆ 4 garlic cloves, minced
- ◆ 2 tablespoons peppers
- ◆ 900g (32 oz.) pork loin roast
- ◆ 1 tablespoon cumin
- ◆ 1 teaspoon oregano
- ◆ 1 tablespoon ground coriander
- ◆ ¾ teaspoon salt
- ◆ ½ white onion, sliced

DIRECTIONS:

1. Place all the ingredients in a freezer bag and cook in a slow cooker on low for between 7 and 8 hours.

2. Serve garnished with cilantro.

Time: 20 minutes

Servings: 8

Calories: 469

Fat: 31g

Protein: 38g

Carbs: 5g

INGREDIENTS:

- ◆ 8 slices of bacon, cooked and chopped
- ◆ 3 garlic cloves, minced
- ◆ 900g (31.7 oz.) Chicken breast, cooked shredded or cubed
- ◆ 455 (16 oz.) spinach, thawed and squeezed to drain well
- ◆ 1 cup Mozzarella cheese, shredded
- ◆ 1 cup Cheddar cheese, shredded
- ◆ ¾ cup ranch dressing

DIRECTIONS:

1. Prepare oven by preheating it to 190 degrees C (375 degrees F).

2. Thaw and squeeze the spinach to drain.

3. In a large bowl, combine the chicken, half the shredded cheese, bacon, spinach, ranch dressing, and garlic and stir well until incorporated.

4. Transfer the mixture into a 9 x13 in (23x33 cm) glass or stoneware casserole dish.

5. Sprinkle the remaining cheddar and mozzarella cheese on top.

6. Bake in the oven for 15 minutes.

7. Serve immediately.

Time: 15 minutes

Servings: 4

Calories: 445

Fat: 31g

Protein: 35g

Carbs: 10g

INGREDIENTS:

For salmon

- ◆ 4 teaspoons Cajun seasoning
- ◆ 170g (6 oz.) (4 pieces) salmon
- ◆ 1 tablespoon oil

For the avocado salsa

- ◆ 2 avocado, diced
- ◆ 1 jalapeno, finely diced
- ◆ 1 tablespoon cilantro, chopped
- ◆ 1 tablespoon lime juice
- ◆ ¼ cup red onion, diced
- ◆ Salt to taste

DIRECTIONS:

1. In a heavy bottom skillet, heat the oil over medium heat.

2. Season the salmon with Cajun and place in skillet with heated oil and cook until slightly blackened and then flip and repeat on the other side.

3. As the salmon cooks, combine all the avocado ingredients in a bowl.

4. Serve the salmon topped with the avocado salsa.

Time: 21 minutes

Servings: 2

Calories: 209

Fat: 57g

Protein: 54g

Carbs: 9g

INGREDIENTS:

- 2 cups cheese, shredded
- 2 cups prepared ground beef, seasoned with Taco
- 2 teaspoons sour cream
- 1 green onion, sliced
- ¼ cup red enchilada sauce, warm in microwave

DIRECTIONS:

1. Prepare oven by preheating it to 175 degree C (350 degrees F) and lay parchment paper on baking sheet.

2. In the sheet pan, arrange the shredded cheese into four separate circles on the pan.

3. Place in the oven and back for 6 minutes until cheese starts to bubble, and the edges of the cheese start to turn brown and remove from the oven.

4. Immediately lay half a cup of ground beef over each, roll the cheese circle around the beef, so you have something that looks like a sausage roll and pour the warm enchilada source over the top.

5. Serve in a plate and add sliced onion and sour cream over the beef enchiladas.

Time: 25 minutes

Servings: 6

Calories: 303

Fat: 20g

Protein: 25g

Carbs: 7g

INGREDIENTS:

- ◆ 680g (24 oz.) pound ham slice
- ◆ 1 head cabbage, medium
- ◆ 2 tablespoons coconut oil
- ◆ ½ chopped yellow onion
- ◆ ½ cup sliced carrots

Optional

- ◆ Garlic
- ◆ Spicy chilli peppers
- ◆ Curry powder
- ◆ Fresh herbs

DIRECTIONS:

1. Chop all the ingredients into bite-size pieces.

2. Add all the ingredients into an instant pot with the coconut oil and cover with water.

3. Simmer for between 3 and 6 hours until cabbage becomes tender, if necessary add more water.

4. Serve immediately of freeze for later use.

Time: 55 minutes

Servings: 12

Calories: 249

Fat: 21g

Protein: 11g

Carbs: 6g

INGREDIENTS:

- ◆ 110g (4 oz.) Organic Cultured Cream Cheese
- ◆ 1 egg, large
- ◆ 1 packet Italian dressing mix
- ◆ 1 cup shredded provolone cheese
- ◆ 1 cup deli meats, chopped
- ◆ 1 ¼ cups almond flour
- ◆ ¼ cup heavy cream
- ◆ ¼ cup water, filtered

DIRECTIONS:

1. Prepare oven by preheating to 175 degrees C (350 degrees F) and grease your muffin pan lightly.

2. In a blender, combine cream cheese, Italian dressing mix, egg, heavy cream, and water and create a smooth blend.

3. In a medium bowl, combine the wet mixture from the blender and the almond flour and mix well.

4. Divide batter into 12 muffin cups.

5. Bake for 20 minutes at 175 degrees C 350 degrees F.

6. Allow the muffins to cool for 5 minutes before transferring to a cooling rack.

7. Serve warm or cold.

Time: 20 minutes

Servings: 6

Calories: 205

Fat: 16 g

Protein: 13 g

Carbs: 1 g

INGREDIENTS:

- ◆ 110g (4 oz.) cooked bacon
- ◆ 12 eggs
- ◆ Salt and pepper to taste

DIRECTIONS:

1. Prepare oven by preheating to 200 degree C (400 degrees F).

2. Put the cake liners in the muffin tins.

3. Into each time, crake one egg and top with any keto-friendly feeling of your choice.

4. Season to taste.

5. Bake until eggs are cooked (about 15 minutes)

6. Placed your cooked bacon on top and serve.

Time: 55 minutes

Servings: 15

Calories: 268

Fat: 24g

Protein: 6g

Carbs: 4g

INGREDIENTS:

Cake

- ◆ 2 cups almond flour
- ◆ 2 tablespoons unflavoured whey protein powder
- ◆ 2 teaspoons baking powder
- ◆ 1 large egg
- ◆ ½ cup sweetener
- ◆ ½ cup butter, melted
- ◆ ½ teaspoon salt
- ◆ ½ teaspoon vanilla extract

Filling

- ◆ 226g (8 oz.) cream cheese, softened
- ◆ 2 large eggs
- ◆ ½ cup butter softened
- ◆ ½ teaspoon vanilla extract
- ◆ ¾ cup powdered Swerve
- ◆ Powdered Swerve for, dusting

DIRECTIONS:

1. Prepare oven by preheating it to 160 degree C (325 degree F) and grease a 9 x13 baking pan lightly.

2. Combine the almond flour, baking powder, protein powder, sweetener, and salt, add the egg, butter, and vanilla extract into the bowl and combine well.

3. Transfer the mixture into the prepared baking pan, leaving some space towards the top.

4. Beat the cream cheese and butter in another bowl into a smooth mixture, beat in the sweetener and combine well, and then beat in the vanilla and eggs to create a smooth mixture

5. Pour the filling on top of the crust and bake for between 35 and 45 minutes, ensuring the filling is set and the centre remains jingle, and the edges are starting to turn golden brown.

6. Take out of the oven and allow to cool and then dust with powdered Swerve and then cut into bars before serving.

Time: 10 minutes

Servings: 4

Calories: 193

Fat: 18g

Protein: 2g

Carbs: 1g

INGREDIENTS:

- ◆ 179g (6 oz.) sugar-free dark chocolate
- ◆ 1 tablespoon Erythritol
- ◆ ½ cup unsweetened almond milk
- ◆ ½ cup heavy cream
- ◆ ½ teaspoon vanilla extract

DIRECTIONS:

1. Over medium heat, in a small saucepan, heat the almond milk, cream and Erythritol and allow to simmer.

2. Remove from heat.

3. Stir in the chocolate and vanilla extract, and whisk continuously until melted.

4. Serve in espresso cups.

For someone starting on a Keto diet, the whole process can look overwhelming, especially if you do not have a diet plan. As a bonus for this book, we are making things easier by suggesting a diet plan you can follow for 14 days and potentially lose 11 pounds. Following a plan ensures that you maintain the discipline of a Keto diet yet still ensuring that your body gets all the nutrients it requires. For each of the 14 days, we will suggest one new recipe, and for the other meals, we will refer you to one of the 50 recipes we have already included in this book.

DAY 1

Breakfast: Egg Muffins (page 18)

Lunch: Lamb and Halloumi Patties

Time: 35 minutes

Servings: 10

Calories: 397

Fat: 33g

Protein: 22g

Carbs: 1g

INGREDIENTS

- ◆ 255g (9 oz.) Halloumi cheese, grated
- ◆ 900g (32 oz.) ground lamb
- ◆ 2 eggs
- ◆ 2 teaspoons cumin, ground
- ◆ 1 tablespoon parsley, finely chopped
- ◆ Pinch of salt and pepper to taste

CUCUMBER CREAM

- ◆ 8 oz. sour cream
- ◆ 3.5 oz. cucumber remove seeds and finely dice
- ◆ 1 teaspoon Cumin

DIRECTIONS:

Patties

1. Mix the patty ingredients in a large bowl.

2. Divide the mix into 10 same size pieces and create a smooth ball from each, and then make burger patties with each ball.

3. Over medium-high heat, grill the patties for between 5 and 8 minutes on each side, until cooked to your liking and then serve with cucumber cream.

Cucumber cream

4. Place all the cucumber cream ingredients in a bowl and mix well, tasting and adjusting seasoning according to your taste.

5. Serve with lamb and Halloumi patties

Dinner: Creamy Chicken Broccoli (page 54)

DAY 2

Breakfast: Keto Breakfast Burrito

Time: 7 minutes

Servings: 1

Calories: 331

Fat: 30g

Protein: 11g

Carbs: 1g

INGREDIENTS:

◆ 2 tablespoons cream, full fat

◆ 2 eggs, medium

◆ 1 tablespoon butter

◆ Herbs and spices (select any keto-friendly)

◆ Salt and pepper to taste

DIRECTIONS:

1. Whisk the eggs, cream, and any spices and herbs.

2. In a frying pan, melt the butter and pour the burrito egg mixture.

3. Spread the burrito egg mixture evenly in the pan, ensuring consistent thinness.

4. Leave to cook for 2 minutes with the lid on and then remove from the heat.

5. Lift the burrito from the frying pan using a spatula and place in a plate.

6. Add the filling of your choice and serve.

Lunch: Frankfurter Risotto (page 36)

Dinner: Keto zucchini pizza boats with goat cheese (page 55)

DAY 3

Breakfast: Keto Matcha Coconut Fat Balls (page 30)

Lunch: Chicken & Cheese Stuffed Peppers (page 37)

Dinner: Keto Chicken Salad with Avocado

Time: 20 minutes

Servings: 2

Calories: 1093

Fat: 80g

Protein: 68g

Carbs: 33g

INGREDIENTS:

Chicken

♦ 4 cloves garlic

♦ 2 boneless chicken thigh fillets

♦ 2 tablespoons olive oil

♦ 1 teaspoon dried thyme

♦ 1 teaspoon salt

♦ 1 teaspoon sweet chilli powder

♦ ½ teaspoon ground black pepper

♦ ¼ cup water

Salad

♦ 2 cups arugula

♦ 2 tablespoons avocado dressing

♦ 1 avocado, sliced

♦ 1 cup purslane leaves

- ◆ 1 tablespoon olives
- ◆ 1 teaspoon nigella seeds
- ◆ 1 teaspoon sesame seeds
- ◆ ½ tablespoon olive oil
- ◆ ½ cup fresh dill
- ◆ Basil leaves
- ◆ A few halved cherry tomatoes

DIRECTIONS:

1. Put the chicken fillets in a skillet, pout in ¼ cup of water and cook them over medium heat with the skillet cover on, heating the pieces until they release their water which you should collect.

2. After removing the water from the skillet, drizzle 2 tablespoons of olive oil over the chicken, add the garlic cloves, salt, black pepper, thyme, and sweet chilli powder and cook covered to a golden brown, flipping the pieces over several times.

3. In a bowl, arrange all the salad ingredients, sprinkle the sesame seeds and nigella seeds over them, and drizzle some avocado oil and olive oil over the salad.

DAY 4

Breakfast: Keto cheese roll-ups

Time: 5 minutes

Servings: 4

Calories: 331

Fat: 30g

Protein: 15g

Carbs: 2g

INGREDIENTS:

- ♦ 225 g (8 oz.) cheddar cheese (use any other keto-friendly cheese of your choice)
- ♦ 50g (1.8 oz.) butter

DIRECTIONS:

1. Slice the cheese pieces on a large cutting board.

2. Slice butter into thin pieces using a knife or a cheese slicer.

3. Cover the cheese slices with butter and roll-up with the butter on the inside.

4. Serve immediately.

Lunch: Keto Taco Salad (page 38)

Dinner: Garlic Rosemary Pork Chops (page 56)

DAY 5

Breakfast: Scrambled Eggs with Mayonnaise (page 19)

Lunch: Slow-Cooked Shredded Beef (page 39)

Dinner: Citrus Salmon en Papillote

Time: 35 minutes

Servings: 6

Calories: 224

Fat: 13g

Protein: 20g

Carbs: 6g

INGREDIENTS:

- ◆ 6 orange slices
- ◆ 6 lime slices
- ◆ 6 salmon fillets (about 110g or 4 ounces each)
- ◆ 3 tablespoons lemon juice
- ◆ 2 tablespoons fresh parsley, minced
- ◆ 1 pound fresh asparagus, trimmed and halved
- ◆ Olive oil cooking spray
- ◆ Salt and pepper to taste

DIRECTIONS:

1. Prepare oven by preheating to 220 degrees C (425 degrees F) and cut parchment into six pieces measuring 15 x10-in and fold into half.

2. Arrange the fish pieces on one half of the parchment and leave the other half free so that you will fold it over the fish,

3. Place the citrus pieces on one side of each piece, top the fish with asparagus, spritz the cooking spray over the fish.

4. Sprinkle the salt, parsley and pepper over the fish and drizzle with lemon juice.

5. Seal the fish inside the parchment and place in the baking pans.

6. Back for 12 to 15 minutes.

7. Take out of the oven and open each packet carefully, allowing the steam to escape before you serve.

DAY 6

Breakfast: Keto Coconut Flour Pancakes (page 20)

Lunch: Shrimp Avocado Salad with Tomatoes and Feta

Time: 20 minutes

Servings: 2

Calories: 430

Fat: 33g

Protein: 24g

Carbs: 12.5g

INGREDIENTS:

- ◆ 227g (8 oz.) shrimp peeled, deveined, patted dry
- ◆ 2 tablespoons salted butter, melted
- ◆ 1 tablespoon olive oil
- ◆ 1 large avocado, diced
- ◆ 1 small beefsteak tomato, diced and drained
- ◆ 1 tablespoon lemon juice
- ◆ 1/3 cup crumbled feta cheese
- ◆ 1/3 cup cilantro or parsley, freshly chopped
- ◆ ¼ teaspoon black pepper ¼ teaspoon salt

DIRECTIONS:

1. Melt butter in a skillet.

2. Toss shrimp into the melted butter until well coated.

3. Heat olive oil in a skillet over medium heat, add the shrimp into the pan creating a single layer and sear for 1 minute before flipping and cooking the shrimp for another minute.

4. Transfer shrimp into a plate and allow to cool as you prepare other ingredients.

5. Add all the other ingredients into a large mixing bowl and toss to mix.

6. Add shrimp and mix before serving.

Dinner: Keto Chicken Enchilada Bowl (page 57)

DAY 7

Breakfast: Asparagus Wrapped in Bacon (page 21)

Lunch: Egg Roll Bowls (page 40)

Dinner: Bake Pesto Chicken

Time: 40 minutes

Servings: 4

Calories: 471

Fat: 22g

Protein: 61g

Carbs: 2g

INGREDIENTS:

- ◆ 226g (8 oz.) mozzarella cheese, thinly sliced or shredded
- ◆ 4 chicken breasts sliced along the centre
- ◆ 3 tablespoons basil pesto
- ◆ ½ teaspoon salt
- ◆ ¼ teaspoon black pepper

DIRECTIONS:

1. Prepare oven by preheating to 175 degree F (350 degrees F).

2. Spray dish with cooking spray and place the chicken in the dish creating a single layer and sprinkle the salt, pepper, and mozzarella cheese on top.

3. Place in the oven and bake for between 35 and 45 minutes watching for the cheese to turn golden brown and bubbly.

4. Serve immediately or later.

DAY 8

Breakfast: Classic Bacon and Eggs (page 25)

Time: 10 minutes

Servings: 4

Calories: 272

Fat: 22g

Protein: 15g

Carbs: 1g

INGREDIENTS:

♦ 150g (5.3 oz.) bacon

♦ 8 eggs

♦ Cherry tomatoes (optional)

♦ Fresh parsley (optional)

DIRECTIONS:

1. Fry bacon over medium heat in a pan until crispy, leave produced fat in the pan, and put the bacon aside.

2. In the same pan, fry the eggs over medium heat, cooking them to the extent you like.

3. Add salt and pepper and then serve with bacon.

Lunch: Low-Carb Keto Meatloaf (page 43)

Dinner: Keto Pizza (page 58)

DAY 9

Breakfast: Keto Sausage Breakfast Sandwich (page 24)

Lunch: Slow Cooker Keto Korean Barbecue Beef

Time: 60 minutes

Servings: 4

Calories: 492

Fat: 21g

Protein: 69g

Carbs: 20g

INGREDIENTS:

- 1360g (48 oz.) boneless beef chuck roast, fat trimmed, cubed
- 2 tablespoons garlic, minced
- 1 tablespoon ginger, freshly grated
- 1 ½ tablespoon hot sauce
- 1 tablespoon spoon sesame oil
- 1 tablespoon apple cider vinegar
- ½ cup low-sodium beef broth
- ½ teaspoon onion powder
- ½ teaspoon pepper
- 1/3 cup golden monk fruit sweetener
- ¼ cup liquid aminos

Add after cooking

- 3 tablespoons green onions, thinly sliced
- 2 tablespoons fresh cilantro, roughly chopped
- 1 ½ teaspoons xanthan gum

DIRECTIONS:

1. Add all ingredients into a freezer bag.

2. Set the slow cooker on high and cook for 4 hours.

3. In increments of ¼ teaspoon, add the xanthan gum and, fold into sauce until sauce thickens.

4. Serve beef bowls with fresh cilantro and green onions as garnish.

Dinner: Bok Choy Chicken Stir Fry (page 59)

DAY 10

Breakfast: Mushroom Spinach Bacon Egg (page 25)

Lunch: Steak with Keto Mushroom Stroganoff (page 44)

Dinner: Keto Ground Beef Casserole (page 52)

Time: 40 minutes

Servings: 8

Calories: 281

Fat: 20g

Protein: 18g

Carbs: 4g

INGREDIENTS:

- 85.5g (3 oz.) cream cheese
- 2 cans green beans, drained
- 453g (16 oz.) ground beef
- ¾ cup mozzarella cheese
- ¾ cup cheddar cheese
- ½ teaspoon garlic powder
- ½ cup broth
- ½ cup heavy whipping cream
- ½ teaspoon pepper
- ½ teaspoon salt

DIRECTIONS:

1. Prepare oven by preheating it to 350 degrees F.

2. In a heavy skillet brown the beef and remove the excess liquid.

3. Add cream cheese into the skillet, stir until melted, and then add the heavy whipping cream, beef broth, salt and pepper, and garlic powder.

4. Allow to boil over medium heat until mixture starts to thicken and then reduce the heat and allow to simmer.

5. When the beef mixture has become thick, add the green beans and sprinkle cheese on top.

6. Move the skillet into the oven and bake for 25 minutes.

7. Serve.

DAY 11

Breakfast: Low Carb Egg in Nest (page 27)

Lunch: Vegan Keto Lo Mein

Time: 10 minutes

Servings: 1

Calories: 195

Fat: 14g

Protein: 5g

Carbs: 4g

INGREDIENTS:

- ◆ 2 tablespoon carrots, shredded
- ◆ 1 package kelp noodles
- ◆ 1 cup frozen broccoli

For the sauce

- ◆ 2 tablespoons tamari
- ◆ 1 tablespoon sesame oil
- ◆ ½ teaspoon garlic powder
- ◆ ½ teaspoon ground ginger
- ◆ ¼ teaspoon Sriracha

DIRECTIONS:

1. Soak kelp noodles in water for a few minutes.

2. In a pan over medium heat toss the sauce ingredients and the broccoli allowing the temperature to increase for about 2 minutes.

3. Drain the water off the noodles and add then into the pan and allow to simmer for a few minutes occasionally stirring the noodles so that they spread out and absorb the sauce.

4. When the noodles have softened turn down the heat and let the dish sit over the dying heat so that the noodles can absorb all the liquid.

5. Serve.

Dinner: Paleo & Keto Chicken Zoodles with Tomatoes (page 60)

DAY 12

Breakfast: Low Carb Breakfast Bowl

Time: 30 minutes

Servings: 1

Calories: 617

Fat: 49g

Protein: 32g

Carbs: 7g

INGREDIENTS:

- ◆ 200 grams (7 oz.) radishes
- ◆ 100g (3.5 oz.) ground sausage
- ◆ 1 large egg
- ◆ ¼ shredded cheddar cheese
- ◆ ¼ teaspoon pink Himalayan salt
- ◆ ¼ teaspoon black pepper

DIRECTIONS:

1. Over medium heat, cook sausage in a pan until fully cooked before removing the sausage from the pan and leaving the grease in the pan.

2. Cut the radishes into bite-size pieces, add into the pan, and season with salt.

3. Cook radishes for 8 to 10 minutes until they are soft enough to pierce with a fork.

4. As the radishes cook, fry the egg to your preference and set aside.

5. When radishes are cooked, place the layer of cooked sausage and cheese and allow the residual heat to melt the cheese.

6. Throw the egg on top and serve warn.

Lunch: Shrimp Ceviche (page 45)

Dinner: Creamy Chicken, Bacon and Cauliflower Bake (page 62)

DAY 13

Breakfast: Ham Steaks with Gruyere, Bacon & Mushrooms (page 28)

Lunch: Keto Caesar Salad

Time: 30 minutes

Servings: 4

Calories: 418

Fat: 35g

Protein: 20g

Carbs: 3g

INGREDIENTS:

- ◆ 141g (5 oz.) Bacon, roughly chopped
- ◆ 4 large Eggs
- ◆ 4 Anchovies, halved
- ◆ 1 large Romaine Lettuce, washed and well-drained
- ◆ 2 servings Keto Croutons
- ◆ 57g (2 oz.) Parmesan cheese shaved
- ◆ 1/3 cup Keto Ceaser Dressing
- ◆ Salt and pepper to taste

DIRECTIONS:

1. Boil eggs over high heat for 12 minutes, and leave in cold water to cool for 10 minutes before peeling and setting aside.

2. Cook bacon over high heat in a skillet until crispy, and drain excess fat and set aside.

3. Break the lettuce into small pieces and place in a serving bowl.

4. Sprinkle cheese over the lettuce.

5. Cut the boiled eggs into half and add to the salad.

6. Drizzle the seasoning and dressing over and toss to mix before serving.

Dinner: Cheeseburger Spaghetti Squash Casserole (page 63)

DAY 14

Breakfast: Peanut Butter Power Granola (page 29)

Lunch: Zesty Chili Lime Keto Tuna Salad (page 48)

Dinner: Keto Ham and Broccoli Creamy Casserole

Time: 10 minutes

Servings: 8

Calories: 397

Fat: 31g

Protein: 24g

Carbs: 6g

INGREDIENTS:

- ◆ 227g (8 oz.) cream cheese, softened
- ◆ 395g (14 oz.) frozen broccoli
- ◆ 2 cups diced ham
- ◆ 1 teaspoon onion powder
- ◆ 1 teaspoon garlic salt
- ◆ 1 cup plain full-fat Greek yoghurt
- ◆ 1 cup crushed pork rinds
- ◆ 1 cup shredded cheese
- ◆ ½ cup mayonnaise
- ◆ ½ teaspoon smoked paprika
- ◆ ¼ teaspoon thyme

DIRECTIONS:

1. Prepare oven by preheating to 175 degree C (350 degree F).

2. In a bowl, mix the ham, thyme, broccoli, rosemary, cream cheese, smoked paprika, yoghurt, basil, onion powder, and garlic.

3. Transfer the casserole mixture into a greased casserole dish.

4. Top the casserole with crushed pork rinds and shredded cheese.

5. Place in the oven and bake for between 45 and 60 minutes or until the casserole starts to brown and bubble.

6. Serve immediately.

Now that you have all the tools you need to start on the Keto diet, you will need to be aware of some tips that will make you succeed.

Prepare: Like everything else in life, the most crucial aspect of the Keto diet is to be adequately prepared. This will assist you in making the decisions about what you will eat easier and prepare for eventualities in advance such as days when you will not be eating at home or times when you are too busy to make your Keto meals.

Balancing the nutrients: The Keto diet is a nutrients game. Hence, you will need to make sure that the foods you eat contain as much fat as possible. Overeating protein, will leave you feeling as if the diet is not helping you meet your goals. It is vital to track the amount of fat, proteins, and carbohydrates you eat every day. This is the reason why we have included this information in all our recipes.

Manage the calories: While calories should not be the only thing you watch, if you eat more calories than your body is burning, you will not lose weight because the weight loss formula is easy: take in fewer calories than you need and lose weight. However, this does not mean that you should eat too little calories. Start by planning your calorie requirements and then preparing meals based on your goals.

Avoid junk food: If you resort to keto versions of junk food sold in fast food outlets, you are essentially subcontracting your goals to someone else. This is the reason why you will need to prepare your meals carefully.

Going on the keto diet is going to be a work in progress, and you will only be able to succeed if you are willing to make the lifestyle changes required to maintain the diet. This means that people around you should understand what you are trying to do so they can lend you the support you need. Whenever the going gets tough, remember the reason why you started in the first place.

EXCLUSIVE BONUS!

Get Keto Audiobook
for FREE NOW!*

The Ultimate Keto Diet Guide 2019-2020:
How to Loose weight with
Quick and Easy Steps

SCAN ME

or go to

www.free-keto.co.uk

DISCLAIMER

Printed in Great Britain
by Amazon

35527918R00066